NEGOTIATION
SKILLS
SIMPLIFIED

Master the art of persuasion, and get what you want without conflict.

Cynthia David

COPYRIGHT

Negotiation skills Simplified © 2024 Cynthia David. All rights reserved.

No part of this publication may be reproduced, distributed, or transmitted in any form or by any means, including photocopying, recording, or other electronic or mechanical methods, without the prior written permission of the author, except in the case of brief quotations embodied in critical reviews and certain other noncommercial uses permitted by copyright law.

CONTENTS

INTRODUCTION 8
   The Importance of Negotiation in Everyday Life 8
   Common Misconceptions About Negotiation 9
   How Mastering Negotiation Can Lead to Better Relationships, Career Success, and Personal Satisfaction. 11
   A Promise to You 13

CHAPTER 1 16
   The Fundamentals of Negotiation 16
   What Is Negotiation? A Simple Definition 16
   Why Negotiation Is Not About Winning or Losing, but Finding Mutual Value. 17
   Types of Negotiation: Everyday Scenarios, from Personal to Professional 18
   The Key Pillars of Successful Negotiation: Preparation, Empathy, and Communication 21

CHAPTER 2 26
   Preparing for Negotiation 26

The Power of Preparation 26
How to Define Your Goals and Know Your Priorities 27
Understanding the Other Party: Researching Their Needs, Desires, and Fears 29
Setting Clear Boundaries—Knowing What You Are Willing to Compromise On 31
Practice Makes Perfect: Preparing Mentally and Emotionally 33

CHAPTER 3 36
Building Rapport and Trust 36
Why Relationships Matter More Than Tactics 36
How to Build Rapport and Trust Before and During Negotiations 37
Active Listening as a Tool for Connection: Letting the Other Party Feel Heard 40
Mirroring: Subtle Techniques to Make the Other Party Comfortable 42
Building a Collaborative, Not Competitive, Environment 45

CHAPTER 4 48

The Art of Persuasion............................48
   Understanding Human Psychology and Decision-Making........................49
   How to Craft Compelling Arguments That Appeal to Logic and Emotion...50
   The Power of Framing: Presenting Your Ideas in a Way That Resonates... 52
   The Use of Storytelling to Make Your Case More Relatable and Persuasive. 54
   The Role of Body Language and Tone in Persuasion.................................56

CHAPTER 5..60
   Managing Conflict and Emotions..........60
   Recognizing the Signs of Tension Before They Escalate.......................61
   How to Stay Calm and Composed During Heated Discussions..............62
   Turning Conflict into Collaboration: How to Address Disagreements Respectfully..64
   Practical Techniques for Defusing Emotionally Charged Situations.......66
   Knowing When to Walk Away:

Recognizing a Dead-End Negotiation.. 69

CHAPTER 6... 72

Finding Win-Win Solutions....................72

The Difference Between Compromise and a Win-Win Outcome...................73

Strategies for Creating Value for Both Sides.. 74

How to Use Creative Problem-Solving to Find Mutually Beneficial Solutions... 76

When and How to Make Concessions Without Losing Ground.................... 78

The Importance of Fairness and How to Ensure Both Parties Feel Satisfied.. 80

CHAPTER 7... 84

Effective Communication in Negotiation... 84

The Role of Clear, Concise Communication in Successful Negotiation... 85

How to Ask the Right Questions to Uncover Hidden Interests.................86

The Art of Phrasing: How to Say "No"

    Without Sounding Harsh................. 87
    Using Silence as a Powerful Negotiation Tool.............................. 89
    How to Clarify Agreements and Avoid Misunderstandings.......................... 90

CHAPTER 8... 94
    Negotiation in Different Contexts.......... 94
        Negotiating at Work: Asking for a Raise, Promotion, or Better Work Conditions.. 95
        Negotiating in Personal Relationships: Reaching Mutual Understanding Without Conflict............................... 96
        Negotiating with Children: Setting Boundaries While Maintaining Harmony..98
        Negotiating with Difficult People: Tactics for Handling Tough Personalities....................................99
        Adapting Your Negotiation Style to Different Cultures and Environments... 101

CHAPTER 9... 104
    Overcoming Common Negotiation Challenges.. 104

Dealing with Aggressive Negotiators: How to Maintain Control... 105

Handling Manipulation: Recognizing and Countering Common Tactics.................... 106

The Fear of Rejection: How to Build Confidence and Overcome Hesitation......108

Managing Time Pressure and Deadlines. 109

How to Keep Negotiations on Track When Things Go Off Course................................ 111

CHAPTER 10..114

Mastering Long-Term Negotiation Success... 114

The Role of Reflection: Learning from Every Negotiation Experience............................ 115

How to Develop a Growth Mindset and Continually Improve Your Skills................ 116

Building Lasting Relationships Through Ethical and Fair Negotiation...................... 118

The Ripple Effect: How Good Negotiation Skills Can Improve Every Area of Your Life... 120

Practical Exercises to Hone Your Negotiation Abilities................................. 122

CONCLUSION..126

Recap of Key Takeaways......................... 126

Start Small, Build Confidence....................128

INTRODUCTION

Negotiation is more than just a tool for business professionals or dealmakers. It's a skill we all use, often without realizing it, in everyday life. Whether you're discussing chores with your partner, convincing your kids to do their homework, or asking for a raise at work, you are negotiating. At its core, negotiation is about communicating your needs and desires while finding a solution that works for everyone involved.

The Importance of Negotiation in Everyday Life

In life, we are constantly in situations where negotiation plays a key role. Imagine trying to agree on where to go for a family vacation, dividing household responsibilities, or even deciding what movie to watch with friends. These are all small but important negotiations.

If you can negotiate effectively, you can avoid unnecessary arguments, build stronger relationships, and create an environment where everyone feels heard. Negotiation also helps us to set healthy boundaries and stand up for ourselves without being confrontational. The better you are at negotiation, the more control you have over your personal and professional life.

Common Misconceptions About Negotiation

Many people think negotiation is only for high-stakes business deals or legal agreements. This couldn't be further from the truth. One of the most common misconceptions about negotiation is that it's only necessary when money is involved or when large decisions are being made. In reality, negotiation happens in everyday situations, big and small. From deciding how to split rent with roommates to resolving a disagreement with a neighbor, negotiation helps smooth over conflicts and ensures everyone's needs are met.

Another misconception is that negotiation has to be aggressive or manipulative, with a clear winner and loser. People often think of negotiation as a battle of wits or a contest of strength. In truth, successful negotiation isn't about overpowering the other person. It's about collaboration—finding common ground and creating solutions where both sides feel satisfied. Good negotiation builds trust, not tension.

How Mastering Negotiation Can Lead to Better Relationships, Career Success, and Personal Satisfaction

When you master negotiation, you improve more than just your ability to close deals—you transform your relationships, your career, and your personal well-being. Here's how:

1. **Better Relationships**: Good negotiation skills can dramatically improve how you relate to others. You'll learn to listen more carefully, understand others' perspectives, and communicate your own needs clearly. This builds trust and respect in both personal and professional relationships. Instead of getting into arguments or power struggles,

you'll find ways to work together towards solutions that make everyone happy.

2. **Career Success**: In the workplace, negotiation is essential. Whether you're asking for a promotion, negotiating your salary, or managing a project with a team, your ability to negotiate can have a direct impact on your success. People who can negotiate effectively tend to be more respected in their jobs because they know how to create win-win situations, lead discussions, and resolve conflicts without drama.

3. **Personal Satisfaction**: When you know how to negotiate, you gain more control over your own life. You can advocate for yourself,

make sure your needs are met, and find balance in situations where you might otherwise feel powerless. Negotiation helps you avoid feelings of resentment or frustration that can come from not getting what you need. Instead, you'll feel empowered and satisfied, knowing you've contributed to a solution that benefits everyone.

A Promise to You

By the end of this book, you will be equipped with practical tools to negotiate effectively without creating tension or conflict. Whether it's negotiating a raise at work, handling a disagreement with a loved one, or making everyday decisions, you'll feel more confident and prepared. You'll learn that negotiation isn't about winning or losing—it's about understanding both your needs and the needs of others, and working together to find the best outcome.

So, let's begin this journey together. You'll soon discover how mastering the art of negotiation can open doors, solve problems, and improve your life in ways you never thought possible. With the right tools and mindset, you'll be ready to negotiate anything—without the stress or conflict that often comes with it.

You may not realize it, but you negotiate every day—whether it's with your boss, your partner, or even yourself. The key to mastering negotiation is believing that you have the power to shape the outcome. Trust your instincts, learn from each experience, and remember that with the right approach, you can achieve more than you ever thought possible.

CHAPTER 1

The Fundamentals of Negotiation

What Is Negotiation? A Simple Definition

At its most basic level, negotiation is a conversation aimed at reaching an agreement between two or more parties. It's the process of discussing needs, wants, or problems and working together to find a solution. Negotiation doesn't always mean haggling over money or making huge deals—it can be as simple as figuring out who's cooking dinner tonight or agreeing on what time to meet friends. In short, negotiation is about finding a common ground where everyone involved feels like their needs are being met.

Why Negotiation Is Not About Winning or Losing, but Finding Mutual Value

One of the biggest misunderstandings about negotiation is the idea that someone has to win, and someone has to lose. Many people go into negotiations thinking, "I have to get what I want," which can create tension, frustration, and even conflict. But in reality, successful negotiation isn't about defeating the other person. It's about finding a solution that works for both sides—a win-win outcome where everyone walks away satisfied.

When you focus on finding mutual value, you're not just looking out for your own interests. You're also trying to understand what the other person needs and how to meet those needs without sacrificing your own goals. By approaching negotiation this way, you create a collaborative atmosphere instead of a competitive one. The goal isn't to "win" but to work together to come up with a solution that benefits everyone. This mindset fosters respect, trust, and long-lasting relationships—whether in personal life or in business.

Types of Negotiation: Everyday Scenarios, from Personal to Professional

Negotiation happens in many areas of our lives, often without us even realizing it. It's not just limited to boardrooms or business deals. Here are some common scenarios where negotiation comes into play:

1. **Personal Relationships**: Whether it's with a spouse, a family member, or a friend, personal negotiation is about balancing each

other's needs and preferences. For example, deciding where to go on vacation, splitting household chores, or figuring out weekend plans all require negotiation. In these cases, the goal is to maintain harmony while ensuring everyone's input is valued.

2. **Workplace Negotiation**: In a professional setting, negotiation might involve discussing your salary, project timelines, or the scope of your responsibilities. But it also includes smaller, everyday interactions like negotiating deadlines, resources, or team roles. At work, strong negotiation skills can help you advance your career, resolve conflicts, and strengthen your professional relationships.

3. **Purchasing and Sales**: Whether you're buying a car, negotiating a rent agreement, or closing a business deal, negotiation plays a key role in any situation where a transaction is taking place. Knowing how to negotiate well in these situations ensures that you get the best value while also maintaining a good relationship with the other party.

4. **Parenting and Family Dynamics**: Parents negotiate with their children all the time, from bedtime routines to homework and chores. Effective negotiation here teaches children responsibility while helping parents maintain structure and boundaries without creating conflict.

In all these cases, negotiation doesn't have to be stressful or difficult. When done right, it simply becomes a conversation aimed at finding a solution everyone can agree on.

The Key Pillars of Successful Negotiation: Preparation, Empathy, and Communication

Successful negotiation relies on three core elements: **preparation, empathy, and communication**. Let's break each one down:

1. **Preparation**

    Before entering any negotiation, it's essential to prepare. This means understanding not only what you want but also what the other person might need or expect. Preparation involves setting clear goals, knowing your limits, and having a plan for how to approach the conversation. For example, if you're negotiating a raise at work, research the industry standards for your position, gather evidence of your accomplishments, and be ready to explain why you deserve more compensation. The better prepared you are, the more confident and composed you'll feel.

2. **Empathy**

Empathy is the ability to put yourself in someone else's shoes. During negotiation, it's important to understand the other person's perspective and acknowledge their feelings and needs. Empathy allows you to approach the conversation with openness and respect, which helps build trust. When people feel heard and understood, they are more likely to cooperate and work towards a solution that benefits both parties. For example, if you're negotiating with a partner about how to spend money, empathizing with their concerns will make it easier to find a financial plan that works for both of you.

3. **Communication**

Clear, respectful communication is the backbone of any successful negotiation. This means being able to express your needs and desires without coming across as demanding or defensive. It also means asking the right questions, actively listening to the other person, and being open to feedback. During a negotiation, how you say something is just as important as what you say. Good communication involves using positive language, staying calm, and focusing on solutions rather than problems.

Understanding the fundamentals of negotiation is the first step toward mastering this vital life skill. Negotiation is about much more than getting your way—it's about finding solutions that work for everyone involved. Whether you're discussing personal matters or handling professional challenges, approaching negotiation with preparation, empathy, and good communication can help you build stronger relationships, achieve your goals, and create lasting solutions.

Negotiation doesn't always mean landing the biggest deal or making the boldest move. Sometimes, the most significant progress comes from small wins—little victories that build your confidence and improve your skills over time. Every time you negotiate successfully, no matter how minor the issue, you're sharpening your abilities and preparing for bigger challenges ahead.

CHAPTER 2

Preparing for Negotiation

The Power of Preparation

In any negotiation, preparation is your most powerful tool. Think of it as building the foundation for success. The more prepared you are, the more confident and focused you'll feel during the negotiation process. When you walk into a negotiation knowing exactly what you want, what the other party might want, and where there's room to compromise, you're in a much stronger position. Preparation allows you to avoid surprises, think clearly under pressure, and make decisions that lead to the best possible outcome.

Without proper preparation, negotiations can quickly become chaotic, with emotions and uncertainties taking control. But with preparation, you can stay calm, navigate through challenges, and guide the conversation toward a solution that works for everyone. In short, preparation transforms you from a passive participant into a proactive negotiator who is in control of the situation.

How to Define Your Goals and Know Your Priorities

Before entering any negotiation, it's crucial to have a clear understanding of what you want to achieve. This might seem obvious, but many people go into negotiations without fully defining their goals. If you don't know what your desired outcome is, it's easy to get sidetracked or settle for less than you deserve.

Start by asking yourself these questions:

- What is my ultimate goal in this negotiation?
- What would be the ideal outcome for me?
- Are there any secondary goals I want to achieve?

For example, if you're negotiating a salary increase, your primary goal might be a specific dollar amount. But your secondary goals might include additional benefits, flexible working hours, or more vacation days. By clearly defining your goals and understanding what's most important to you, you'll be able to stay focused during the negotiation and avoid unnecessary distractions.

It's also important to rank your priorities. Not all of your goals will carry the same weight. Know which goals are must-haves and which ones you are more flexible on. This will help you make decisions during the negotiation and know when to stand firm or when to compromise.

Understanding the Other Party: Researching Their Needs, Desires, and Fears

Negotiation isn't just about what you want—it's about understanding the other person's perspective as well. The more you know about the other party's needs, desires, and fears, the better prepared you'll be to find common ground.

Start by researching the other person or organization. Ask yourself:

- What are their goals in this negotiation?
- What challenges or concerns might they have?
- What would make them feel satisfied with the outcome?

For example, if you're negotiating a job offer, research the company's financial health, its culture, and the job market for your role. Understanding what the company values (like teamwork or long-term commitment) and what it might be worried about (such as budget constraints or employee turnover) can help you tailor your negotiation strategy.

When you take the time to understand the other party's perspective, you demonstrate empathy and respect. This not only makes them more likely to cooperate but also helps you avoid misunderstandings or conflicts. Negotiation is not a battle; it's a conversation. Knowing what the other side wants allows you to craft solutions that meet both your needs and theirs.

Setting Clear Boundaries—Knowing What You Are Willing to Compromise On

While it's important to know your goals, it's equally important to set clear boundaries. Boundaries are the limits you are not willing to cross. These are the areas where you won't compromise, no matter what. Setting boundaries helps you protect your interests and ensures that you don't give up too much just to reach an agreement.

For example, if you're negotiating a business deal, your boundary might be a minimum price you're willing to accept. If the other party can't meet that price, you know that it's time to walk away. Having clear boundaries keeps you from feeling pressured into accepting an unfavorable deal.

At the same time, it's helpful to know what areas you *are* willing to compromise on. Not all aspects of the negotiation will be equally important to you, so identify the areas where you can be flexible. This might include things like deadlines, additional perks, or minor details. Being open to compromise shows that you're cooperative and solution-oriented, which makes it easier to reach a favorable agreement.

Practice Makes Perfect: Preparing Mentally and Emotionally

Finally, one of the most important aspects of preparation is getting yourself mentally and emotionally ready for the negotiation. Negotiations can be stressful, especially when important things are at stake. To perform well under pressure, it's essential to practice and build confidence before the actual conversation.

Here are a few ways to prepare mentally and emotionally:

1. **Visualization**: Picture yourself in the negotiation. Imagine how the conversation might unfold, the challenges that might arise, and how you'll handle them. Visualizing success can boost your confidence and

make the real negotiation feel more familiar and manageable.

2. **Role-Playing**: Practice negotiating with a friend or colleague. Take turns playing both sides of the conversation, and experiment with different strategies. Role-playing helps you anticipate possible scenarios and develop responses so that you're not caught off guard during the actual negotiation.

3. **Stay Calm**: Negotiations can sometimes become heated or emotional, especially when there's a lot on the line. It's important to stay calm and composed. Practice deep breathing or other relaxation techniques that can help you remain level-headed during

difficult moments. Emotional preparation is just as important as intellectual preparation.

Preparation is the cornerstone of successful negotiation. When you take the time to clearly define your goals, understand the other party's perspective, set firm boundaries, and mentally prepare yourself, you put yourself in the best possible position to achieve a positive outcome. Negotiation is not about outsmarting the other person or winning at all costs—it's about finding a solution that works for everyone involved.

CHAPTER 3

Building Rapport and Trust

Why Relationships Matter More Than Tactics

When it comes to negotiation, many people focus solely on tactics and strategies, thinking that's the key to getting what they want. However, successful negotiation is about more than clever tactics. It's about relationships. People are more likely to work with you, compromise, and find mutual solutions if they trust you and feel a connection.

Think of negotiation as a partnership, not a battle. You and the other party are both working toward a solution that benefits everyone. When you approach the situation with trust and mutual respect, it opens the door for honest communication, reduces misunderstandings, and paves the way for creative solutions. In contrast, if you treat the negotiation like a game to be won, it's likely to create tension, distrust, and a competitive atmosphere that can backfire.

Building rapport and trust should be your priority in every negotiation. Strong relationships lead to better deals, smoother conversations, and long-term partnerships, whether you're negotiating in your personal life or professional setting.

How to Build Rapport and Trust Before and During Negotiations

1. **Be Genuine**: Trust starts with being authentic. People can quickly sense when someone is not being sincere, and that can

create distance. Whether you're negotiating a raise, a business deal, or a personal agreement, be yourself and communicate honestly. If the other person feels that you're being straightforward and fair, they are more likely to respond in kind.

2. **Find Common Ground**: Before diving into the details of the negotiation, take a moment to connect on a personal level. This can be as simple as finding shared interests, asking how their day is going, or talking about mutual acquaintances. Building small, personal connections helps to humanize the conversation and reminds both parties that they're working together, not against each other.

3. **Respect Cultural and Personal Differences**: Everyone approaches negotiations differently, and this can be influenced by culture, personality, or experience. Some people may prefer to take a formal approach, while others might be more relaxed. Pay attention to the other party's style and adjust your approach accordingly. Showing respect for their preferences can help establish trust from the beginning.

4. **Be Open and Transparent**: Hiding your intentions or being overly secretive can lead to suspicion and make the other person hesitant to trust you. Be open about your goals, your priorities, and your concerns.

Transparency builds trust, and when both parties feel that they're being honest with each other, it creates a collaborative environment.

Active Listening as a Tool for Connection: Letting the Other Party Feel Heard

One of the most powerful tools in negotiation is active listening. It's not just about hearing what the other person is saying—it's about fully understanding their concerns, desires, and perspective. When you listen actively, you show that you value their input, and this makes them feel respected and heard.

Here are a few ways to practice active listening:

- **Pay full attention**: Put away distractions, maintain eye contact, and focus on the speaker. This shows that you're genuinely interested in what they have to say.
- **Reflect back what you hear**: Summarize or paraphrase their points to confirm you understand. For example, you might say, "So, what I'm hearing is that you're concerned about the timeline, correct?"
- **Ask clarifying questions**: Don't be afraid to ask questions if something is unclear. This not only shows that you're engaged but also helps you avoid misunderstandings later on.
- **Acknowledge their emotions**: Sometimes, people just want to feel understood, especially if emotions are involved. Saying

something like, "I can see why that would be frustrating for you" helps validate their feelings and build rapport.

Active listening makes the other party feel valued, which in turn makes them more open to working with you. It also helps prevent conflict by ensuring that both sides fully understand each other before making decisions.

Mirroring: Subtle Techniques to Make the Other Party Comfortable

Mirroring is a subtle but effective technique to help build rapport during a negotiation. It involves subtly reflecting the other person's behavior, tone, or body language to create a sense of connection. When done naturally, mirroring can make the other person feel more comfortable and relaxed, as it signals that you're in sync with them.

Here's how you can apply mirroring in a negotiation:

- **Match their tone**: If the other person is speaking calmly and quietly, try to match that tone. If they are more energetic, let your energy reflect theirs. This helps you build rapport and makes the conversation feel more harmonious.
- **Body language**: Pay attention to their body language and try to reflect it in subtle ways. For instance, if they lean forward while speaking, you might do the same. If they

smile, return the smile. This creates a sense of comfort and familiarity.

- **Language and phrasing**: Use similar language or phrases that the other person is using. For example, if they describe something as "challenging," you can refer to it in the same way during your response. This builds a subconscious bond and makes the other party feel understood.

While mirroring can be effective, it's important not to overdo it. The goal is to create a natural flow in the conversation, not to mimic them exactly. When used properly, mirroring helps you build a connection and puts both parties at ease.

Building a Collaborative, Not Competitive, Environment

A key element of successful negotiation is shifting the mindset from competition to collaboration. Too often, people approach negotiation as a win-lose situation, where one side must get the upper hand. This type of thinking leads to tension, distrust, and conflict. Instead, aim to create a collaborative environment where both parties work together to find a solution that benefits everyone.

Here are some ways to build a collaborative environment:

- **Use "we" language**: Instead of framing the negotiation in terms of "I" versus "you," focus on the collective goal. Use phrases like "Let's figure out a solution together" or "How can we make this work for both of us?" This shifts the focus from individual gain to mutual benefit.

- **Encourage brainstorming**: Collaboration thrives when both sides feel free to suggest ideas and explore possibilities. Encourage the other party to share their thoughts and work together to come up with creative solutions that meet both your needs.
- **Focus on shared interests**: Identify areas where your goals overlap. When both parties recognize that they have common interests, it's easier to build trust and work together. For example, if you're negotiating a business deal, you both likely want to build a successful partnership—focusing on that

shared interest can help guide the conversation in a positive direction.

When you create a collaborative environment, negotiation becomes less about winning and more about finding a solution that works for everyone. This leads to better outcomes, stronger relationships, and less conflict.

Building rapport and trust is the foundation of any successful negotiation. By focusing on relationships over tactics, listening actively, using subtle techniques like mirroring, and fostering a collaborative environment, you can create a positive atmosphere where both sides feel respected and heard. With trust at the core, negotiations become smoother, more productive, and less stressful.

CHAPTER 4

The Art of Persuasion

Persuasion is an essential skill in negotiation. It's about more than just getting someone to agree with you—it's about guiding them to see things from your perspective and helping them understand why your ideas or solutions make sense. Mastering the art of persuasion involves understanding how people think and what motivates them to make decisions. It's about using the right words, emotions, and nonverbal cues to make your case compelling.

Understanding Human Psychology and Decision-Making

At the core of persuasion is human psychology. People are not always driven by cold, hard facts. Emotions, biases, and personal experiences play a huge role in the decisions they make. To persuade effectively, you need to recognize that people are complex and that their choices are influenced by both logic and emotion.

For example, someone might be reluctant to agree with a business proposal because they feel uncertain or anxious about the risks involved. In this case, providing more data or evidence might not be enough. You'll need to acknowledge their emotions and address their concerns on an emotional level before they can even begin to consider the logical points you present.

By understanding what motivates people—whether it's fear, desire, or a sense of security—you can tailor your arguments to address both their emotional and logical needs. This makes your persuasion efforts more effective and builds a deeper connection with the other person.

How to Craft Compelling Arguments That Appeal to Logic and Emotion

A good argument doesn't rely on logic alone; it speaks to the heart as well as the mind. When crafting your case, it's important to strike a balance between the two.

1. **Start with logic**: Present your facts clearly. Explain why your idea or solution makes sense from a practical standpoint. For example, if you're negotiating a raise, you might start by laying out your achievements, showing how they've contributed to the company's success, and providing industry standards for salary increases.

2. **Appeal to emotions**: Once you've established the logical foundation, connect with the other person on an emotional level. For instance, you could talk about your passion for the job, your dedication, and how receiving a raise would allow you to continue growing within the company. Emphasize

shared values or mutual goals, as this helps the other party feel invested in the outcome.

People are more likely to be persuaded when they feel emotionally connected to your argument, so always consider how your message might resonate with their feelings and concerns.

The Power of Framing: Presenting Your Ideas in a Way That Resonates

Framing is the way you present your ideas or position to make them more appealing. It's not about changing the facts, but about choosing the right perspective or angle to highlight what matters most to the other person.

For example, imagine you're negotiating a deal with a client. Instead of focusing on how the deal benefits you, frame it in terms of how it benefits them. Highlight how your product or service will solve their problems, save them time, or increase their profits. By framing your offer in a way that aligns with their needs and priorities, you make it more compelling.

Another way to use framing is by emphasizing potential losses rather than gains. Studies show that people are often more motivated by the fear of losing something than by the prospect of gaining something new. So, if you're negotiating with someone who's hesitant, you might frame the conversation around what they stand to lose if they don't take action, rather than just focusing on the potential benefits.

Effective framing can shift the way someone views a situation, making them more likely to agree with your perspective.

The Use of Storytelling to Make Your Case More Relatable and Persuasive

Stories are powerful tools in persuasion because they engage both the logical and emotional sides of the brain. Unlike statistics or data, which can feel dry and abstract, stories are relatable and memorable. They help people see the human side of an issue and make your argument more concrete.

When you tell a story, you create a connection with your listener. You're not just presenting facts—you're painting a picture that makes your case come alive.

For example, if you're negotiating with a team on a new project proposal, instead of just listing the advantages of your approach, you might share a story about how a similar project you worked on led to great success. Describe the challenges you faced, how you overcame them, and the positive impact it had. This makes your argument more engaging and helps the other party visualize the benefits of your proposal.

When telling a story:

- **Keep it relevant**: Make sure the story directly supports your argument.
- **Be concise**: Don't lose your listener with unnecessary details.

- **Include emotion**: Share how you felt during the events of the story, as this helps create an emotional connection.

The Role of Body Language and Tone in Persuasion

Persuasion isn't just about what you say—it's also about how you say it. Your body language and tone of voice play a crucial role in how your message is received.

1. **Body language**: Nonverbal cues, such as eye contact, gestures, and posture, can either reinforce or undermine your message. If your words say one thing but your body says another, people will trust what they see more than what they hear. For example, crossing your arms or avoiding eye contact

can make you seem defensive or untrustworthy. On the other hand, maintaining an open posture and making eye contact conveys confidence and sincerity.

2. **Tone of voice**: Your tone of voice can convey confidence, enthusiasm, or doubt. If you speak too softly or with hesitation, you may come across as unsure, even if your argument is strong. A steady, confident tone shows that you believe in what you're saying, which makes it easier for others to believe in it too.

Here are a few tips for using body language and tone to your advantage in negotiation:

- **Be aware of your posture**: Stand or sit up straight, and avoid crossing your arms or legs.
- **Maintain eye contact**: This shows that you're engaged and confident.
- **Use gestures to emphasize points**: But avoid overdoing it, as too many gestures can be distracting.
- **Match your tone to the situation**: If you're discussing a serious issue, keep your tone calm and measured. If you're excited about a new opportunity, let that enthusiasm come through in your voice.

Mastering the art of persuasion is about understanding how people think and using that knowledge to present your ideas in a way that resonates. By crafting arguments that appeal to both logic and emotion, framing your points effectively, using storytelling to connect with your audience, and paying attention to your body language and tone, you can become a more persuasive negotiator.

CHAPTER 5

Managing Conflict and Emotions

Negotiation can often bring up strong emotions and conflicts, but learning how to manage these situations effectively can make the difference between success and failure. While it's natural for disagreements to arise, especially when both parties have different goals, handling them with grace and respect is key to maintaining productive discussions. In this chapter, I'll explore how to manage conflict and emotions, ensuring that you stay in control and keep the negotiation on track.

Recognizing the Signs of Tension Before They Escalate

One of the most important skills in managing conflict is recognizing when tension is building. This gives you the opportunity to address the situation before it escalates into a full-blown argument. Some common signs of tension include:

- **Changes in tone or body language**: If the other person's voice becomes sharp or their posture shifts to something more closed off (like crossed arms), it may indicate frustration or defensiveness.
- **Interruptions or raised voices**: If someone begins to talk over you or speak more loudly, it's a signal that emotions are starting to rise.

- **Long pauses or silence**: When the other party suddenly becomes quiet, it might be because they're processing something they disagree with or are feeling overwhelmed.

By staying attuned to these signals, you can intervene early and steer the conversation in a more positive direction. A simple acknowledgment like, "I sense there's some frustration—can we take a moment to clarify any concerns?" can help prevent tensions from boiling over.

How to Stay Calm and Composed During Heated Discussions

Staying calm during heated negotiations is crucial for keeping things productive. When emotions flare up, it's easy to react impulsively, which can derail the entire process. Here are some strategies to help you remain composed:

1. **Take deep breaths**: It might sound simple, but taking a few slow, deep breaths can calm your nervous system and help you stay centered.
2. **Pause before responding**: When the conversation gets heated, resist the urge to respond immediately. Take a moment to collect your thoughts before speaking. This pause allows you to choose your words carefully rather than reacting emotionally.
3. **Focus on the issue, not the person**: Avoid taking things personally. If the other party becomes upset, remind yourself that their frustration is likely tied to the situation, not

you as an individual. Keeping this perspective can help you avoid becoming defensive.

By maintaining your composure, you set the tone for the negotiation, making it easier to steer the conversation back to a constructive path.

Turning Conflict into Collaboration: How to Address Disagreements Respectfully

Conflict doesn't have to mean the end of a negotiation. In fact, when handled correctly, it can lead to better solutions. The key is to approach disagreements as opportunities for collaboration rather than as battles to win.

- **Acknowledge the other person's perspective**: One of the most effective ways to defuse conflict is to show that you understand the other party's concerns. Phrases like, "I can see why you feel that way," or "That's a valid point" demonstrate respect for their viewpoint, even if you don't fully agree.

- **Focus on common goals**: Instead of framing the negotiation as a win/lose scenario, emphasize the shared objectives. For example, if you're negotiating a contract, you might say, "We both want this partnership to be successful. Let's find a way to make that happen."
- **Offer solutions, not just objections**: When disagreements arise, instead of just pointing out problems, propose solutions. For

instance, if you can't meet a proposed deadline, offer an alternative timeline that works for both parties. This shows that you're committed to finding a middle ground.

By addressing conflict with respect and collaboration in mind, you can transform what could be a sticking point into a step toward a stronger agreement.

Practical Techniques for Defusing Emotionally Charged Situations

In some cases, emotions can run high, making it difficult to have a rational discussion. Here are some practical techniques to calm the situation and refocus the conversation:

1. **Acknowledge feelings**: If the other party is clearly upset, it can help to acknowledge their emotions. Simply saying, "I can tell this is frustrating," or "I understand this is important to you," can help them feel heard and may diffuse some of their anger.

2. **Take a break**: If things are getting too heated, don't hesitate to suggest a short break. A few minutes away from the negotiation can allow both parties to cool down and return with a clearer perspective. You can say something like, "Why don't we take a quick break and come back in 10 minutes to continue?"

3. **Use neutral language**: When emotions are high, it's important to avoid language that

could escalate the situation further. Instead of saying, "You're wrong," try, "I see it differently," or, "Let's look at this from another angle." This keeps the conversation focused on the issue rather than personal attacks.

4. **Maintain an open posture**: Body language can either calm or intensify a situation. Keep your posture open and relaxed—avoid crossing your arms or leaning forward aggressively. A calm demeanor signals that you are open to resolving the conflict in a respectful way.

By using these techniques, you can help de-escalate emotionally charged situations and create space for productive dialogue.

Knowing When to Walk Away: Recognizing a Dead-End Negotiation

Sometimes, despite your best efforts, a negotiation reaches a dead end. It's important to recognize when it's time to walk away rather than forcing a deal that isn't in your best interest. Here are some signs that a negotiation might be at a dead end:

- **Unreasonable demands**: If the other party refuses to budge on demands that are unrealistic or unfair, it may be time to reconsider the negotiation.
- **Lack of compromise**: A negotiation is built on give-and-take. If the other side shows no willingness to compromise or meet you halfway, there may be no path forward.

- **Repeated cycles of conflict**: If the conversation keeps circling back to the same disagreements without progress, it could indicate that the parties are too far apart in their goals.

When walking away, do so gracefully. You don't want to burn bridges, as there might be opportunities to revisit the negotiation later. You can say something like, "It seems we're not able to find common ground at this time. Perhaps we can revisit this discussion in the future when circumstances change."

Knowing when to walk away is a valuable skill that protects your interests while keeping the door open for future opportunities.

Managing conflict and emotions in negotiation is a delicate balancing act, but with the right approach, you can navigate even the most difficult discussions. By recognizing the signs of tension, staying calm, turning conflict into collaboration, and knowing when to step back, you can keep negotiations productive and respectful.

In any negotiation, emotions can run high, but the key to success is keeping a clear head. When you stay calm, you're able to think more clearly, communicate more effectively, and find solutions that benefit everyone involved. Remember, negotiation is not a battle; it's a conversation. Breathe, stay focused, and let your calm presence guide you to a positive outcome.

CHAPTER 6

Finding Win-Win Solutions

In any negotiation, the ultimate goal isn't just to "win" or make the other party give in to your demands. Instead, it's about finding a solution that works for both sides—a win-win outcome. This kind of agreement doesn't leave one party feeling like they've lost or sacrificed too much, but rather, both walk away satisfied and positive about the outcome. Let's explore what it means to achieve a win-win solution, how to create value for both sides, and how to approach concessions in a way that benefits everyone involved.

The Difference Between Compromise and a Win-Win Outcome

Many people think compromise is the same as a win-win solution, but they're actually quite different. Compromise usually means both sides give up something to meet in the middle. While this can be effective in certain situations, it often leaves both parties feeling like they lost something. A win-win outcome, on the other hand, goes beyond simply meeting in the middle—it involves finding a solution that satisfies both parties' main interests.

For example, let's say you're negotiating the price of a service. Instead of one party lowering their price and the other paying more than they want, a win-win solution might involve adding extra value, such as offering additional services or extending the contract. In this case, both sides feel they've gained something without making painful sacrifices.

Strategies for Creating Value for Both Sides

The key to a win-win solution is creating value for both sides. This requires thinking beyond the immediate demands and exploring ways to satisfy each other's deeper needs. Here are a few strategies to help you create value in negotiations:

1. **Understand the other party's priorities**: Before you can find a win-win solution, you need to know what truly matters to the other side. Ask open-ended questions to get a clear picture of their goals, concerns, and motivations. For example, they might care more about quality than cost, or they might

be more focused on time than specific details. The better you understand their priorities, the more effectively you can craft a solution that meets both of your needs.

2. **Look for trade-offs**: In many negotiations, each party values different aspects of the deal. By identifying what's more important to each side, you can make trade-offs that allow both parties to get what they want without either feeling like they've lost. For instance, you could offer flexibility in one area (like timelines) if the other party is willing to concede in another (like price).

3. **Think outside the box**: Win-win solutions often require creative thinking. Don't be afraid to propose ideas that go beyond the

obvious options. If you can brainstorm new ways to meet both parties' interests, you'll increase the chances of finding a solution that leaves everyone satisfied. For example, if a client is reluctant to pay your full rate, you might offer a discount in exchange for a longer-term contract or a referral.

How to Use Creative Problem-Solving to Find Mutually Beneficial Solutions

Creative problem-solving is an essential tool for achieving win-win outcomes. It's about looking for solutions that may not be immediately obvious and thinking beyond the limits of a typical negotiation. Here's how you can use creative problem-solving to find mutually beneficial solutions:

- **Explore all possibilities**: During the negotiation, don't focus on a single solution. Instead, brainstorm multiple ways to approach the issue. Ask "What if...?" and explore different angles until you find something that works for both sides.
- **Look for common ground**: Even when you and the other party seem to be at odds, there are usually shared interests that can serve as a foundation for creative solutions. Focus on what you both want to achieve and work from there. For example, both parties might agree on the importance of a long-term partnership, even if they're disagreeing over specific terms in the short term.

- **Consider non-monetary solutions**: Not every solution has to involve money or pricing. Sometimes, offering something like additional support, flexibility, or other perks can satisfy the other party's needs without directly impacting your bottom line. These creative offers can often bridge the gap in difficult negotiations.

When and How to Make Concessions Without Losing Ground

In any negotiation, there will be times when you have to make concessions. But the key is to do so without losing ground or feeling like you've given up too much. Here's how to make smart concessions that still keep the negotiation moving toward a win-win outcome:

1. **Prioritize your concessions**: Know ahead of time what areas you are willing to be flexible in and what aspects are non-negotiable. This will help you give ground in the right places while still protecting your main interests.
2. **Make concessions conditional**: If you're going to make a concession, try to link it to a concession from the other party. For example, "I'm willing to lower the price, but in exchange, I'd like a longer contract term." This keeps the balance of power even and ensures that both parties are making progress toward a mutually beneficial solution.

3. **Frame concessions positively**: Instead of framing concessions as sacrifices, position them as benefits that you're offering to help move the negotiation forward. This helps maintain a positive atmosphere and shows the other party that you're focused on finding a solution that works for both sides.

The Importance of Fairness and How to Ensure Both Parties Feel Satisfied

Fairness is at the heart of any successful negotiation. Both parties need to feel like they've been treated fairly, or resentment can linger and undermine the agreement. Here's how you can ensure fairness and leave both sides feeling satisfied:

- **Be transparent**: Open communication builds trust. Share relevant information openly and honestly, and encourage the other party to do the same. This creates an environment where both parties feel comfortable sharing their concerns and working toward a fair solution.

- **Keep long-term relationships in mind**: Even if you're negotiating a one-time deal, think about the long-term impact. How the negotiation is handled will affect future interactions and partnerships. If both parties feel the agreement was fair, it sets the stage for future collaboration and mutual respect.

- **Check in with the other party**: Throughout the negotiation, periodically check in with the other side to ensure they feel the process is fair. Simple questions like, "How are you feeling about where we're at?" or "Is there anything you'd like to address before we move forward?" can help identify and resolve any lingering concerns before they become major issues.

Finding win-win solutions is about creating value for both sides and ensuring that everyone leaves the table feeling satisfied. By understanding the difference between compromise and a true win-win, using creative problem-solving, making strategic concessions, and focusing on fairness, you can turn even the toughest negotiations into successful agreements. Remember, a successful negotiation isn't about one side winning—it's about both sides feeling like they've gained something valuable.

It's easy to get caught up in the details during a negotiation, but never lose sight of the bigger picture. What do you really want to achieve? How can you create value for both parties? When you focus on long-term goals instead of immediate wins, you're more likely to find solutions that work for everyone and build lasting relationships in the process.

CHAPTER 7

Effective Communication in Negotiation

In any negotiation, effective communication is key. How you express your thoughts, ask questions, and respond to the other party will determine whether the negotiation moves toward a positive outcome or hits a wall. Clear and concise communication helps avoid misunderstandings, ensures that both sides are on the same page, and builds trust. Let's look at how to communicate effectively during a negotiation, how to ask questions that uncover hidden interests, and how to use techniques like silence and careful phrasing to your advantage.

The Role of Clear, Concise Communication in Successful Negotiation

Clear communication is the foundation of any successful negotiation. When you clearly state what you want, why you want it, and what you're willing to offer, it reduces the chances of miscommunication and confusion. The other party is more likely to understand your position and respond appropriately when you communicate concisely.

Being concise doesn't mean being blunt or leaving out details—it means delivering your message in a way that's easy to understand. Focus on the key points of the negotiation, avoid going off-topic, and be direct without being confrontational.

For example, instead of saying, "I think I might be okay with this offer, but I'll need to check with my team, and I'm not sure if we can get this done in time," try, "I'm open to this offer, but I need to confirm it with my team. Let's discuss a realistic timeline."

How to Ask the Right Questions to Uncover Hidden Interests

In negotiations, what people say they want is often only the surface of their true desires. To find out what really matters to the other party, you need to ask the right questions. These are not yes-or-no questions but open-ended ones that encourage deeper discussion.

For example, instead of asking, "Is this price acceptable to you?" you could ask, "What concerns do you have about this price?" or "How can we adjust this offer to better meet your needs?" These kinds of questions allow the other party to explain their thoughts and priorities more fully, which can help you find solutions that address their underlying interests.

By uncovering these hidden interests, you're better positioned to craft an agreement that works for both sides. This also builds trust, as it shows you're genuinely interested in meeting their needs, not just pushing your own agenda.

The Art of Phrasing: How to Say "No" Without Sounding Harsh

Negotiation often involves saying "no" to certain demands, but how you say it can make a big difference. If you reject a proposal too bluntly, it may come across as dismissive or aggressive, potentially damaging the relationship or escalating tension. Instead, focus on phrasing your "no" in a way that leaves room for continued dialogue.

One effective way to say "no" without sounding harsh is to acknowledge the other party's position and offer an alternative. For example, instead of saying, "No, I can't do that," you could say, "I understand where you're coming from, but I'm afraid that option won't work for us. However, here's what we could do instead." This keeps the conversation open and positions you as being flexible and solution-oriented.

Another approach is to frame your "no" around your limitations or constraints, rather than outright refusal. For example, "Unfortunately, I'm unable to meet that deadline, but I can commit to delivering by the end of the week. Would that work for you?"

Using Silence as a Powerful Negotiation Tool

Silence is often an overlooked yet powerful tool in negotiation. People tend to feel uncomfortable with silence and rush to fill it, which can lead them to reveal more information or make concessions. Using silence strategically can give you an advantage by allowing you to observe the other party's reactions and encouraging them to speak more openly.

For example, after making a proposal, don't rush to justify or explain it further. Let the silence hang for a moment, and allow the other party to consider your offer. They might start sharing more of their thoughts or even offer a counterproposal that's more favorable to you.

Similarly, if the other party makes a demand that seems unreasonable, you can pause for a moment before responding. The silence can create pressure, leading them to rethink or soften their position.

How to Clarify Agreements and Avoid Misunderstandings

Misunderstandings can derail even the best-intentioned negotiations, which is why it's crucial to clarify agreements as you go. This means repeating back what you've agreed on in clear terms, asking questions if something is unclear, and making sure both sides are aligned before moving forward.

After each key point is discussed, summarize what's been agreed on to ensure there are no discrepancies. For example, you might say, "Just to confirm, we're agreeing that delivery will be by Friday, correct?" This allows both parties to verify that they're on the same page.

It's also important to clarify any vague language or assumptions. If the other party says, "We need this done soon," ask for specifics: "When exactly would you need it by?" This prevents misunderstandings about timelines, expectations, or commitments.

In addition to verbal clarifications, putting agreements in writing is an essential step to avoid any confusion later. A written agreement ensures that both parties have a clear reference to the terms discussed and agreed upon, reducing the risk of future disputes.

Effective communication is the backbone of successful negotiation. By clearly expressing your needs, asking the right questions, and using tools like silence and thoughtful phrasing, you can navigate even the most challenging negotiations with confidence. Remember, negotiation isn't just about talking—it's about truly understanding the other party and making sure that both sides are heard and respected.

The secret to becoming a great negotiator lies in your ability to listen. When you truly hear what the other person is saying, you can understand their needs, address their concerns, and find common ground. Listening not only builds trust but also gives you the insights you need to offer solutions that work for everyone. So, speak less and listen more—it's one of the most powerful tools in negotiation.

CHAPTER 8

Negotiation in Different Contexts

Negotiation is not limited to formal business meetings or high-stakes deals—it's something we engage in every day, often without even realizing it. Whether you're asking for a raise at work, reaching an agreement with a loved one, or dealing with a difficult person, negotiation skills are crucial. In this chapter, I'll explore how to negotiate effectively in various situations, from the workplace to personal relationships. I'll also look at how to adjust your approach depending on the personalities involved or the cultural context.

Negotiating at Work: Asking for a Raise, Promotion, or Better Work Conditions

Negotiating at work can feel intimidating, but it's an essential part of career growth. Whether you're asking for a raise, promotion, or improved work conditions, preparation and clear communication are key. The first step is to define your goals and gather evidence to support your case. **For example**, if you're asking for a raise, be prepared to discuss your achievements, how they've contributed to the company, and how your value has grown over time.

When negotiating for a promotion, emphasize the new responsibilities you're ready to take on and explain how this move benefits both you and the organization. It's important to frame the conversation in a way that highlights mutual value—not just what you want, but how it benefits the company as well.

Timing also matters. Be mindful of the company's current situation, such as budget constraints or major projects, and choose a moment when your request is likely to be well-received.

Negotiating in Personal Relationships: Reaching Mutual Understanding Without Conflict

Negotiation in personal relationships is about reaching mutual understanding without causing conflict or resentment. Whether you're discussing household chores, making financial decisions, or planning how to spend time together, it's important to approach these conversations with empathy and a willingness to listen.

In personal relationships, negotiation isn't about "winning" or getting everything your way. Instead, focus on finding solutions that work for both parties. Use "I" statements to express your needs without blaming the other person. For example, instead of saying, "You never help around the house," you could say, "I feel overwhelmed by the chores and would appreciate more help."

Listening is crucial. Make sure your partner feels heard, and try to understand their perspective before offering solutions. Building rapport and trust in these conversations can help prevent misunderstandings and create a healthier, more collaborative relationship.

Negotiating with Children: Setting Boundaries While Maintaining Harmony

Negotiating with children can be challenging, as they often have strong opinions and limited patience. However, negotiation with kids is important for teaching them about boundaries, compromise, and problem-solving. The key is to strike a balance between being firm and flexible, allowing them to express their opinions while also maintaining clear boundaries.

One effective tactic is to offer choices within acceptable limits. For example, instead of saying, "You need to clean your room now," you could say, "Would you like to clean your room before or after dinner?" This gives them a sense of control while still accomplishing the goal.

It's also important to explain the reasons behind your requests in a way they can understand. When children feel heard and respected, they are more likely to cooperate and less likely to rebel against rules.

Negotiating with Difficult People: Tactics for Handling Tough Personalities

We all encounter difficult people at some point—whether they're aggressive, stubborn, or simply unwilling to compromise. Negotiating with tough personalities requires patience, emotional control, and strategic thinking.

One of the most effective tactics is to remain calm and composed, even when the other person is being difficult. Responding with anger or frustration will likely escalate the situation. Instead, use active listening to acknowledge their concerns, even if you disagree. This can help de-escalate tension and make the other party feel understood.

Another approach is to focus on the facts, not emotions. Difficult people often rely on emotional arguments, but you can steer the conversation back to objective points by presenting facts, data, or logical reasoning. Additionally, setting clear boundaries from the start helps prevent the other party from taking advantage of the situation.

In cases where the person refuses to budge, consider whether it's worth continuing the negotiation or if it's better to walk away. Sometimes, the best negotiation strategy is recognizing when it's a dead-end and saving your time and energy.

Adapting Your Negotiation Style to Different Cultures and Environments

In today's globalized world, we often find ourselves negotiating across different cultures, each with its own unique customs and communication styles. What works in one cultural context may not work in another, so it's essential to adapt your negotiation style based on the environment.

For example, in some cultures, direct communication is valued, and it's expected that people will clearly state their needs and desires. In other cultures, indirect communication is more common, and negotiations may be approached with subtlety, with an emphasis on preserving relationships and saving face.

Before entering a negotiation in a different cultural context, it's important to research the cultural norms and expectations. Pay attention to factors such as how much emphasis is placed on hierarchy, how people handle disagreements, and whether decisions are made quickly or slowly. Adapting to these differences can help you build trust and rapport, making the negotiation more likely to succeed.

Negotiation is a skill that applies to every area of life, from work to personal relationships. By adapting your approach to fit different contexts—whether you're negotiating with a boss, a family member, a child, or a difficult person—you can achieve better outcomes without conflict. Understanding the unique dynamics of each situation and tailoring your communication style accordingly is the key to mastering negotiation in any context.

CHAPTER 9

Overcoming Common Negotiation Challenges

Negotiation doesn't always go smoothly. At times, you'll face tough challenges that test your patience, skills, and confidence. Whether you're dealing with aggressive negotiators, manipulation, or time pressure, staying calm and composed is key. In this chapter, I'll explore common obstacles in negotiation and how you can overcome them effectively. By the end, you'll have the tools to handle even the most difficult negotiations with confidence.

Dealing with Aggressive Negotiators: How to Maintain Control

Aggressive negotiators can be intimidating. They may try to dominate the conversation, interrupt, or make demands without considering your position. However, just because someone is aggressive doesn't mean you have to lose control of the negotiation.

One of the best strategies is to stay calm. If you react emotionally, it may escalate the situation, making it harder to reach a resolution. Instead, focus on maintaining your composure and redirecting the conversation back to the facts. Acknowledge their points, but firmly state your own. For example, you can say, "I understand your perspective, but here's why this approach works better for both of us."

It's also helpful to set boundaries early on. Let the other party know what behavior is acceptable and what's not. If they're being overly pushy, politely but firmly remind them of the goal—to find a solution that works for both sides.

Handling Manipulation: Recognizing and Countering Common Tactics

Manipulative tactics are common in negotiations. These can range from exaggerating facts to using guilt or pressure to make you concede. It's important to recognize when someone is trying to manipulate you so you can respond appropriately.

One common tactic is the "good cop, bad cop" routine, where one negotiator is friendly while the other is aggressive. This is designed to make you side with the "good cop" and give in more easily. When you recognize this, remain neutral and stick to your objectives.

Another tactic is creating false urgency, where the other party claims there's limited time or opportunity. In this situation, ask for proof or details about the urgency. Don't rush into a decision without fully understanding the facts.

The key to handling manipulation is to question anything that feels off or too one-sided. Politely ask for clarification or more information, and never feel pressured to agree if something doesn't align with your goals.

The Fear of Rejection: How to Build Confidence and Overcome Hesitation

The fear of rejection can be a major obstacle in negotiation. Many people hesitate to ask for what they want because they're afraid of being turned down or appearing unreasonable. However, negotiation is a normal process, and hearing "no" is not the end of the road—it's an opportunity to keep the conversation going.

Building confidence starts with preparation. The more prepared you are, the more comfortable you'll feel when presenting your case. Know your value, be clear about what you want, and have facts to back up your request. This makes it easier to stand your ground, even if the initial response isn't positive.

Another way to overcome the fear of rejection is to reframe how you think about "no." Instead of seeing it as a failure, view it as a step in the negotiation process. A "no" can often open the door to further discussion, giving you a chance to adjust your approach or present alternatives.

Managing Time Pressure and Deadlines

Negotiations often come with deadlines, which can create stress and lead to rushed decisions. Time pressure may be used intentionally by the other party as a tactic to get you to agree to terms you're not fully comfortable with.

To manage time pressure, always plan ahead. If you know a deadline is approaching, give yourself enough time to prepare thoroughly. During the negotiation, prioritize the most important points first, so if time runs out, you've covered the key areas.

If the other party is pushing for a decision before you're ready, it's okay to ask for more time. For example, you can say, "I need a little more time to think this over and ensure we're making the best decision for both sides." This shows that you're being thoughtful and considerate, which is a sign of a good negotiator.

When deadlines are tight, it's crucial to stay focused on your goals. Avoid getting sidetracked by less important issues and keep the conversation moving toward a resolution.

How to Keep Negotiations on Track When Things Go Off Course

Negotiations can sometimes take unexpected turns, whether it's due to miscommunication, changing demands, or emotional outbursts. When this happens, it's easy to lose track of the original goals and get caught up in side issues.

To keep things on track, it's important to regularly remind both parties of the main objective. If the conversation veers off course, gently steer it back by saying something like, "Let's refocus on the issue at hand." This helps prevent distractions from derailing the negotiation.

Active listening is another essential tool. By truly hearing the other party's concerns and addressing them directly, you can avoid misunderstandings and keep the negotiation moving forward.

Finally, if things get heated, it may be helpful to take a break. Stepping away from the conversation for a few minutes or even a day can give both sides a chance to cool down and come back with a clearer perspective.

Challenges in negotiation are inevitable, but they don't have to stop you from reaching a successful outcome. Whether you're facing an aggressive negotiator, dealing with manipulation, or battling your own fear of rejection, there are strategies you can use to stay in control. By managing time pressure and keeping the conversation on track, you can overcome obstacles and guide the negotiation toward a positive result.

Not every negotiation will go perfectly, and that's okay. Sometimes, you won't get exactly what you wanted, but that doesn't mean you've failed. Instead, treat setbacks as lessons—reflect on what worked, what didn't, and how you can improve next time. Each time you bounce back, you're one step closer to mastering the art of negotiation.

CHAPTER 10

Mastering Long-Term Negotiation Success

Negotiation is not just a one-time event. To truly become a skilled negotiator, you need to view it as an ongoing learning process. Each negotiation—whether it's a small conversation or a major deal—is an opportunity to reflect, grow, and build lasting relationships. In this chapter, I'll explore how you can master long-term negotiation success by learning from your experiences, developing a growth mindset, and applying ethical negotiation practices that benefit you in every aspect of life.

The Role of Reflection: Learning from Every Negotiation Experience

After every negotiation, no matter how big or small, it's essential to take time to reflect on what happened. Think about what went well and what could have been improved. Did you achieve your goals? Were there moments where the conversation got off track? What strategies worked best for you, and where did you feel unsure?

Reflection helps you understand your strengths and weaknesses, allowing you to fine-tune your approach for the next time. By analyzing your experiences, you'll start to notice patterns in your negotiation style and those of others. This insight will help you become more aware of how to adapt in future situations.

A simple practice is to write down a few key takeaways after each negotiation. Ask yourself:

- What did I learn?
- How did the other party respond to my points?
- What could I have done differently to achieve a better outcome?

This ongoing reflection helps you continually sharpen your skills and become more confident.

How to Develop a Growth Mindset and Continually Improve Your Skills

A growth mindset is the belief that you can always improve through effort and learning. In negotiation, this mindset is crucial for long-term success. Instead of seeing mistakes or challenges as failures, view them as opportunities to grow and improve.

To develop a growth mindset in negotiation:

1. **Embrace challenges**: Don't shy away from difficult negotiations. Each one is a chance to practice and get better.
2. **Learn from feedback**: If you receive constructive criticism from others or notice your own mistakes, take it as valuable information that can help you improve.
3. **Stay curious**: Continually seek new knowledge about negotiation techniques, communication strategies, and human behavior. The more you learn, the more

versatile you'll become in various negotiation settings.

By adopting this mindset, you'll be more open to experimenting with new approaches and refining your skills over time.

Building Lasting Relationships Through Ethical and Fair Negotiation

One of the hallmarks of a successful negotiator is the ability to build long-term relationships. While winning a single negotiation might feel like a victory, true success comes from creating connections that last. This is where ethical and fair negotiation practices come into play.

Ethical negotiation means being honest, transparent, and respectful throughout the process.

It's about aiming for outcomes where both parties feel satisfied, rather than trying to manipulate or take advantage of the other side.

When you negotiate ethically:

- You build trust, which can lead to more opportunities in the future.
- People are more likely to want to work with you again.
- You establish a positive reputation that will serve you in both personal and professional life.

By focusing on fairness and mutual benefit, you'll create relationships that extend far beyond the negotiation table. These relationships can open doors, foster collaboration, and enhance your influence in various aspects of life.

The Ripple Effect: How Good Negotiation Skills Can Improve Every Area of Your Life

Mastering negotiation doesn't just benefit you in business deals or formal settings. It has a ripple effect that can improve every area of your life. When you're a skilled negotiator, you can:

- **Improve your personal relationships**: Whether it's negotiating household responsibilities, resolving conflicts, or reaching mutual decisions, your relationships will become stronger and more balanced.
- **Advance your career**: Good negotiation skills can help you secure raises,

promotions, better working conditions, or new opportunities.

- **Achieve personal goals**: From buying a house to planning a trip, negotiation plays a role in reaching agreements that suit your needs and desires.

As you develop your abilities, you'll find that negotiation becomes a natural part of how you communicate and navigate challenges. You'll feel more empowered to advocate for yourself while also maintaining healthy, positive relationships with others.

Practical Exercises to Hone Your Negotiation Abilities

To continue growing as a negotiator, it's important to practice regularly. Here are a few exercises that can help you refine your skills:

1. **Role-Playing**: Find a partner and simulate different negotiation scenarios, such as asking for a raise, resolving a conflict, or bargaining over a purchase. Practice both sides of the negotiation to understand different perspectives.

2. **Mind Mapping**: Before entering a negotiation, create a mind map of your goals, possible outcomes, and the other party's likely interests. This will help you stay organized and clear about your objectives.

3. **Active Listening Practice**: During everyday conversations, practice active listening by focusing completely on the other person's words, asking clarifying questions, and summarizing what they've said. This skill is crucial for effective negotiation.
4. **Daily Reflections**: After each negotiation or important conversation, jot down a few reflections on what went well and what could be improved. Over time, you'll notice patterns and areas for growth.
5. **Silence Challenge**: In your next negotiation, practice using silence after presenting a point or asking a question. This can encourage the other party to speak more

and reveal additional information, which you can use to your advantage.

Mastering long-term negotiation success requires continuous effort, reflection, and practice. By learning from every experience, adopting a growth mindset, and prioritizing ethical negotiation, you can build lasting relationships and improve various areas of your life. The skills you develop will empower you to navigate challenges with confidence and poise, leading to more satisfying outcomes in both your personal and professional worlds.

As you move forward, keep practicing, stay curious, and remember that negotiation is not just about getting what you want—it's about finding solutions that work for everyone involved. With these tools, you're well on your way to becoming a negotiation master.

Perfection is not the goal—progress is. Becoming a skilled negotiator doesn't happen overnight, and it's okay to make mistakes along the way. What matters is that you keep showing up, keep practicing, and keep learning. Persistence is what will ultimately lead you to success, no matter how many bumps you encounter on the road.

CONCLUSION

As you've worked your way through this book, you've learned the key principles, tools, and techniques of negotiation. From understanding the fundamentals to mastering persuasion, handling conflict, and finding win-win solutions, you now have a solid foundation to negotiate confidently and effectively. But becoming a master negotiator is not just about understanding the theory; it's about applying these skills in real-life situations, big and small.

Recap of Key Takeaways

Let's quickly recap some of the most important lessons from the book:

- **Negotiation is not about winning or losing**: It's about finding value for both sides and creating solutions that benefit everyone involved.
- **Preparation is your strongest weapon**: Knowing your goals, the other party's interests, and setting clear boundaries are essential to successful negotiation.
- **Building rapport and trust** is key to effective negotiation: Relationships matter, and creating a collaborative environment leads to better outcomes.
- **Persuasion is an art**: By appealing to both logic and emotion, framing your ideas effectively, and using body language, you can make your case more compelling.

- **Conflict doesn't have to be negative**: With the right techniques, you can turn disagreements into productive conversations and maintain harmony.
- **Clear communication** is the backbone of any successful negotiation: Asking the right questions, listening actively, and ensuring everyone is on the same page will help you avoid misunderstandings.
- **Negotiation is everywhere**: Whether at work, in personal relationships, or even with children, negotiation is a skill you can apply in all areas of life.

Start Small, Build Confidence

While these lessons are powerful, it's natural to feel a bit overwhelmed when you think about applying them. The key is to start small. Begin by practicing your skills in everyday negotiations—whether it's asking for a discount at a store, discussing household responsibilities, or resolving a minor disagreement with a friend. The more you practice, the more comfortable and confident you'll become.

Remember, negotiation is a skill that improves over time. Every conversation, whether a success or a challenge, is a learning opportunity. So don't be afraid to make mistakes. Reflect on each experience, and use it to grow stronger in your next negotiation.

Even the most experienced negotiators never stop learning. Negotiation is an evolving skill, and each situation presents new challenges and opportunities for growth. Keep honing your abilities by staying curious, seeking out new strategies, and adapting to different people and contexts.

Practice is key to mastering negotiation. The more you engage in it, the more natural it will become. Over time, you'll develop the instincts and techniques needed to handle any negotiation with ease, turning potential conflicts into opportunities for mutual understanding and success.

Now that you've equipped yourself with these valuable tools, it's time to take action. Whether it's asking for that well-deserved raise, negotiating better terms in a contract, or simply improving communication in your personal relationships, you have the power to negotiate for the life you want—without conflict.

Approach each negotiation with confidence, knowing that you have the skills to create positive outcomes for yourself and others. Trust in your ability to listen, empathize, and find solutions that leave everyone feeling satisfied.

Your journey to becoming a master negotiator doesn't end with this book—it's just the beginning. As you apply these principles and sharpen your skills, you'll find that negotiation is not just about getting what you want; it's about building better relationships, creating value for all parties, and living a more empowered, fulfilling life.

So go out there and put these tools to use. With each negotiation, you're not just improving your own life—you're also learning how to navigate the world with confidence, clarity, and compassion. The power is in your hands to shape your future, one conversation at a time.

www.ingramcontent.com/pod-product-compliance
Lightning Source LLC
Chambersburg PA
CBHW050305230526

45471CB00005B/2022